Prayer Therapy

Prayer Therapy

written by
Keith McClellan, O.S.B.

illustrated by
R.W. Alley

ONE
CARING
PLACE

Abbey Press

Text © 1990 by Keith McClellan, O.S.B.
Illustrations © 1990 St. Meinrad Archabbey
Published by One Caring Place
Abbey Press
St. Meinrad, Indiana 47577

Library of Congress Catalog Number
89-82664
ISBN 0-87029-225-0

Printed in the United States of America

Foreword

Do you ever wish you were closer to God? Do you sometimes feel a twinge of guilt for neglecting prayer? Do you envy the people who seem to have it all together? Do you long for peace and stillness of heart?

Many people today think they cannot pray. They view praying as a special gift of church activists, the elderly, or saints. Because they are busy, they too readily dismiss the prayer possibilities that surround them. These individuals have not learned to appreciate their own God-given talent for praying.

If you are among these people—or if you just need encouragement for your ongoing prayer journey—take heart! The pages of *Prayer Therapy* offer simple but age-old wisdom to inspire you with new confidence and conviction.

Real prayer is organic—it grows out of your own life, personality, needs, and rhythms. Each day and every moment are filled with opportunities for prayer. If we seize these moments, we open ourselves to the greatest enrichment—and most effective therapy—possible.

Prayer isn't for specialists; prayer is for you and for me. May the following pages lead you to the One who satisfies every prayerful heart.

1.

Prayer begins in a restless heart. Listen to its stirring.

2.

Prayer is a yearning for one's true home. Follow its lead.

3.

Prayer is like a garden. Tend it and it will be fruitful.

4.

Don't worry about words or formulas. Prayer is a listening.

5.

Prayer has many methods.
Do it your own way.

6.

Pray always, but schedule special times too. The spirit, like the body, needs formal exercise.

7.

Let your prayer be short.
Love needs few words.

8.

Pray where you are.
God is everywhere.

9.

If you <u>need</u> something, pray for it. God desires your good.

10.

If you <u>want</u> something, ask yourself, "Do I want what God wants?" God wants your true good.

11.

Remember: your work and struggles are not unholy. Pray and God will come to you just as you are.

12.

When your praying becomes dry and routine, keep at it. Parched earth welcomes the rain.

13.

Bring your anger to prayer.
Hot metal can be molded.

14.

When God seems far away,
keep praying. Light can be
blinding.

15.

When you sin and continue to fail, pray anyway. God keeps on loving you.

16.

Pray when you're worried.
Prayer puts everything in
perspective.

17.

If, for any reason, you cannot pray, relax. The desire to pray is already a prayer.

18.

When prayer invites you
to take risks, have courage.
God will uphold you.

19.

When you feel sad or sorry,
weep. Tears are a prayer of
the heart.

20.

If you don't like somebody,
pray for them. Prayer reveals
the hidden God.

21.

When you receive bad news, take heart. Praying uncovers the spark in the cinders.

22.

When sickness, age, pain, or worry steals your concentration, relax. God is an understanding friend.

23.

If you begin to feel advanced in the ways of prayer, think again. God's life runs deeper than your feelings or experiences.

24.

If prayer makes you passive and indifferent, it isn't prayer. True prayer will bear fruit in care and service.

25.

Use quiet times for prayer. Silence draws you to the Infinite.

26.

Use noisy times for prayer.
Sound is the clamor of creation
seeking God.

27.

Pray when you feel lonely.
Prayer puts you in the company
of angels.

28.

When life is cruel and unjust,
keep praying. God is the victim,
not the cause.

29.

Touch the joys and troubles of
your friends and neighbors.
Shared life is a shared prayer.

30.

When your heart is bursting with thanks, just be. God's spirit is praying within you.

31.

When you are overawed before Mystery, just be. God's spirit is praying within you.

32.

Embrace the whole world
in your prayer. Peace depends
on it.

33.

Pray in your resting. Sleep is the prayer of a creature secure in God's love.

34.

Pray in your rising. Each dawn draws you closer to the Light.

35.

To pray is to breathe. Do it deeply and you will be filled with life.

Keith McClellan is a member of St. Meinrad Archabbey, a Benedictine monastery in southern Indiana.

Illustrator for the Abbey Press Elf-help Books, **R.W. Alley** also illustrates and writes children's books. He lives in Barrington, Rhode Island, with his wife, daughter, and son.

The Story of the Abbey Press Elves

The engaging figures that populate the Abbey Press "elf-help" line of publications and products first appeared in 1987 on the pages of a small self-help book called *Be-good-to-yourself Therapy*. Shaped by the publishing staff's vision and defined in R.W. Alley's inventive illustrations, they lived out author Cherry Hartman's gentle, self-nurturing advice with charm, poignancy, and humor.

Reader response was so enthusiastic that more Elf-help Books were soon under way, a still-growing series that has inspired a line of related gift products.

The especially endearing character featured in the early books—sporting a cap with a mood-changing candle in its peak—has since been joined by a spirited female elf with flowers in her hair.

These two exuberant, sensitive, resourceful, kindhearted, lovable sprites, along with their lively elfin community, reveal what's truly important as they offer messages of joy and wonder, playfulness and co-creation, wholeness and serenity, the miracle of life and the mystery of God's love.

With wisdom and whimsy, these little creatures with long noses demonstrate the elf-help way to a rich and fulfilling life.

Elf-help Books . . . adding "a little character" and a lot of help to self-help reading!

Take-charge-of-your-life Therapy
(new, improved binding)
#20168-1 $4.95   ISBN 0-87029-271-4

Self-esteem Therapy (new, improved binding)
#20165-7 $4.95   ISBN 0-87029-280-3

Work Therapy (new, improved binding)
#20166-5 $4.95   ISBN 0-87029-276-5

Everyday-courage Therapy
#20167-3 $3.95   ISBN 0-87029-274-9

Peace Therapy
#20176-4 $3.95   ISBN 0-87029-273-0

Friendship Therapy
#20174-9 $3.95   ISBN 0-87029-270-6

Christmas Therapy (color edition)
#20175-6 $5.95   ISBN 0-87029-268-4

Grief Therapy
#20178-0 $3.95   ISBN 0-87029-267-6

More Be-good-to-yourself Therapy
#20180-6 $3.95   ISBN 0-87029-262-5

Happy Birthday Therapy
#20181-4 $3.95   ISBN 0-87029-260-9

Forgiveness Therapy
(new, improved binding)
#20184-8 $4.95   ISBN 0-87029-258-7

Keep-life-simple Therapy
#20185-5 $3.95   ISBN 0-87029-257-9

Be-good-to-your-body Therapy
#20188-9 $3.95   ISBN 0-87029-255-2

Celebrate-your-womanhood Therapy
#20189-7 $3.95   ISBN 0-87029-254-4

Acceptance Therapy (color edition)
#20182-2 $5.95   ISBN 0-87029-259-5

Acceptance Therapy (regular edition)
#20190-5 $3.95   ISBN 0-87029-245-5
Keeping-up-your-spirits Therapy
#20195-4 $3.95   ISBN 0-87029-242-0
Play Therapy
#20200-2 $3.95   ISBN 0-87029-233-1
Slow-down Therapy
#20203-6 $3.95   ISBN 0-87029-229-3
One-day-at-a-time Therapy
#20204-4 $3.95   ISBN 0-87029-228-5
Prayer Therapy
(new, improved binding)
#20206-9 $4.95   ISBN 0-87029-225-0
Be-good-to-your-marriage Therapy
(new,improved binding)
#20205-1 $4.95   ISBN 0-87029-224-2
Be-good-to-yourself Therapy (hardcover)
#20196-2 $10.95   ISBN 0-87029-243-9
Be-good-to-yourself Therapy
(new, improved binding)
#20255-6 $4.95   ISBN 0-87029-209-9

Available at your favorite bookstore or directly from us at
One Caring Place, Abbey Press Publications, St. Meinrad,
IN 47577.

Phone orders: Call 1-800-325-2511.